Big Ben

Although they searched for nearly an hour there was no trace of Sheba.

"It's getting really cold," Julie said, pulling her anorak hood up. She looked up at the sky. "Look at those clouds."

Neil looked. The sky was heavy with yellow-grey snow clouds. His heart sank.

"If it snows, that poor little dog won't stand a chance," he said. "She's clipped. She doesn't have any coat to keep her warm."

Visions of Sheba lying shivering and injured filled their minds. Neil looked at the lead-coloured river. "I'm beginning to hope she *has* been stolen," he said. "At least she'd be safe."

Titles in the Puppy Patrol series

More Puppy Patrol stories follow soon

Puppy Patrol
Big Ben

Jenny Dale

Illustrated by
Mick Reid

A Working Partners Book
MACMILLAN CHILDREN'S BOOKS

Special thanks to Helen Magee

First published 1997 by Macmillan Children s Books
a division of Macmillan Publishers Limited
25 Eccleston Place, London SW1W 9NF
Basingstoke and Oxford
www.macmillan.co.uk

Associated companies throughout the world

Created by Working Partners Limited
London W6 0QT

ISBN 0 330 34906 6

13 15 17 19 18 16 14 12

A CIP catalogue record for this book is available from
the British Library.

Typeset in Bookman Old Style
Printed and bound in Great Britain by Mackays of Chatham plc, Kent

Chapter One

"Hey," said Chris Wilson. "What are you stopping for?"

Neil Parker pointed into a garden. "Look at that!" he said.

Chris braked and came to a stop. He rubbed his hands together as a sudden gust of wind blew across from the playing fields of Meadowbank School. "What's wrong?"

Neil was off his bike and walking towards one of the houses on the other side of Jarvis Road. Their big back gardens were in full view. Chris followed him. There was a large grey and white dog tied to a tree in the nearest garden. As they

1

approached, it lifted its head and howled.

"What a rotten thing to do to a dog," said Neil. "The poor animal must be absolutely miserable to howl like that. We should check it out."

"If I'm late for tea one more time this week, Neil, I won't get any," Chris said.

"We can't just ignore it," said Neil. "It could be hurt."

Chris sighed. He knew it was no good arguing with Neil when there might be a dog in trouble. Neil was mad about dogs. His parents ran a boarding kennels and rescue centre just outside Compton.

"Wait a minute! That's old Mr Taylor's house," Chris said suddenly.

"I didn't know he had a dog," Neil said.

"He doesn't," said Chris. "And anyway, he's in Manchester staying with his daughter. Mum says he hasn't been very well recently and he needed a rest. That house is falling apart. He's too old to look after it properly."

Chris's mum was a district nurse in Compton and seemed to know everything about everybody.

"So if the house is empty, who tied up the dog?" Neil said. "And when? The poor thing could be starving! We've got to do something. I just don't believe anybody would do that to a dog."

Chris looked into the back garden of Mr Taylor's house. The dog was huge and hairy. Chris shivered in the wind.

"At least it won't be cold, not with that coat," he said.

The dog raised its enormous shaggy head again and let out a howl.

"Ouch!" said Chris. "That hurt. What a gigantic dog!"

"It's a bobtail," Neil said. "An Old English sheepdog."

The dog lowered its head and shook it from side to side as if trying to shake itself free from the rope attached to its collar. It had a beautiful white head and forequarters with grey on its back and hind legs. It really was big – even for an Old English sheepdog.

"Isn't it magnificent?" said Neil. "It's got the classic blue-grey coat and it must be nearly seventy-five centimetres at the shoulder."

"Fascinating, Neil, but what is it doing in Mr Taylor's garden?" Chris said.

"Maybe he's back. Maybe he got a dog to keep him company," Neil said.

"He wouldn't get a great big thing like that," said Chris. "He'd get something small – like Mrs Fitz's poodle next door."

Neil knew all about Mrs Fitz. Her real name was Mrs Fitzherbert but they all called her Mrs Fitz – not that she knew that! She had a pedigree toy poodle called

Sheba of Sharendon. She kept the little animal neatly groomed and clipped and hated any other dogs going anywhere near Sheba.

"Uh-oh," said Chris. "Guess who's just looked out of her window?"

Neil dragged his eyes away from the dog and looked at the house next door. Mrs Fitzherbert was standing at the window with a frown on her face. She was holding her poodle in her arms. As they watched, she made shooing motions.

"I think she wants us to go," Chris said.

But Neil stood his ground. "And leave the bobtail?" he said. "We can't do that. What if somebody tied it up there because they knew the house was empty? What if it's been abandoned?"

Neil stretched out a hand and the sheepdog stopped howling. The dog turned its great furry head towards Neil and trotted over to the gate. It could only just reach by pulling the rope tight. Neil leant over the gate and gave the dog a pat, rubbing its ears. The sheepdog nuzzled back, its huge tongue lolling.

"He's fantastic," said Neil. "How could anybody tie him up? We've got to rescue him. We can't leave him here with the house empty."

"The house *isn't* empty," said Chris. "Look!"

Neil looked up. Someone was moving around upstairs. He could see the figure of a woman quite clearly against the uncurtained windows.

"Maybe it's Mr Taylor's daughter," said Chris. "Maybe the dog belongs to her."

Neil's mouth set in a firm line. "Well, if he is her dog," he said, "all I can say is she doesn't deserve him."

There was a tapping sound and Chris looked round. "It's Mrs Fitz again," he said. "We'd better go."

For a moment Neil didn't want to move. He gave the dog a last pat and looked it over carefully.

On close inspection, the bobtail didn't seem to have been badly treated in any other way. Its coat was thick and well-groomed. Neil knew that grooming an Old English sheepdog wasn't easy. So *some-*

body had been taking good care of the bob-tail.

Quickly, Neil ran a hand over the dog's ribs. He was lean but not thin under his heavy coat. Neil parted the hair that drooped over the dog's face. Two bright, intelligent eyes looked up at him. The dog's nose felt moist and his tongue was clean and unfurred. He licked Neil's hand and gave a deep, resonant bark.

"It's OK, boy," Neil said. "I'll find out what's going on. Nobody is going to tie you up like this if I can help it."

"Are you coming?" Chris asked. He shivered as another gust of icy wind ruffled his hair. "I'm starving and it's freezing cold! Come on, Neil."

Neil stepped back. "OK," he said. "But I'm going to ask Mum and Dad about this. You can't just keep a dog tied up like that. There must be a law against it."

The dog howled again as Neil and Chris walked away.

Chris looked back. "Ow!" he said. "That would drive anybody mad."

Neil looked at the window of the house

next door. Mrs Fitzherbert was looking daggers at the Old English sheepdog.

"Mrs Fitz doesn't seem to be enjoying it much either," said Chris.

Neil gave him a look. "So what do you think it feels like for the dog?" he said. "*He's* the one that's tied up. Even with a thick coat he'll get cold in weather like this."

"OK, OK, keep your hair on," said Chris. He grinned. "And, anyway, that dog is going to be all right."

"How do you know?" said Neil.

"Don't be daft," Chris said. "Of course he's going to be all right. The Puppy Patrol are on the case!"

Neil grinned back in spite of his anxiety. Everybody who knew Neil and his family called them the "Puppy Patrol". They were always riding around Compton in the King Street Kennels Range Rover with its logo on the doors.

Neil and Emily, his nine-year-old sister, had already brought several poor mistreated animals into the rescue centre. In fact, Sam, the family pet, had been abandoned as a puppy. He had been brought to the rescue centre four years ago when Neil was only seven.

Sam was a Border collie and very clever. Neil spent a lot of time on Sam's agility training. There was a big dog show coming up in a few weeks' time in Manchester and he really wanted to enter Sam in the Agility event.

Sarah, Neil's younger sister, was only five. She was more interested in her hamster, Fudge. But for Neil, it was dogs, dogs and more dogs. His greatest ambition was to work with dogs when he grew up.

Neil didn't get a chance to talk to his parents about the bobtail until after tea. Emily came in from school in a really bad mood.

"You'll never guess," she said, dropping her schoolbag on the kitchen floor and bending down to give Sam a cuddle.

The black and white Border collie licked her face enthusiastically.

"What?" said Mrs Parker, laying the table for tea. "Emily, don't dump your bag in the middle of the floor like that."

Mr Parker opened the oven door. "I'm making you a vegetarian lasagne tonight so I hope you're all hungry," he said.

"Has it got broccoli in it?" said Sarah from under the table.

"What are you doing under there?" asked Mrs Parker.

"I'm seeing what it's like for Sam," said Sarah. "He sits under the table when we're eating."

Carole Parker ran a hand through her short dark hair. "I'm living in a madhouse," she said.

Bob Parker took the lasagne out of the

oven and put it on the worktop. He peered under the table.

"There isn't any broccoli in it," he said to Sarah. "Come on or you won't hear what Emily has to tell us."

Emily came back from dumping her schoolbag on the hall floor instead of the kitchen floor.

"Ugh!" she said, sitting down beside Neil. "What a day! There's a new girl in our class. Her name is Julie Baker and I have to look after her."

"I like new people," said Sarah.

"She's a real moaning Minnie," Emily said. "All she can talk about is the friends she used to have and how much she's going to miss them."

"She'll make new friends," said Mrs Parker, dishing out the food.

"Not if she goes on like this, she won't," said Emily. "And then there's Ben."

"Who's Ben?" asked Neil.

Emily took a mouthful of food and shook her head. "I don't know," she said, "but *he's* really unhappy as well. He misses their old house."

11

"That must be her brother," Sarah said. "If we ever moved from here I would hate it – and so would Fudge. And Sam. Wouldn't you, Sam?"

Sam looked up from under the table and gave a short bark.

"We would all hate it," said Neil.

Emily looked thoughtful for a moment, then she sighed. "I *was* a bit unsympathetic," she said. "I'll try harder tomorrow."

"Good for you," Bob Parker said. "It must be really difficult moving to a new school in the middle of term."

"Why don't you ask her to tea?" said Carole Parker.

"What? In a madhouse?" Mr Parker joked.

Sarah looked round the table. "I *like* living in a madhouse," she said. "And so does . . ."

"Fudge!" said everybody else.

Chapter Two

Neil got a chance to talk to his dad when they went out to the kennels after tea.

The boarding kennels ran along two sides of the courtyard in the grounds of the Parkers' house. In between the two kennel blocks was a store and feeding station and behind the house was a field where Neil would set up Sam's practice Agility course.

Kate McGuire, the kennel maid, had already fed and watered the dogs but Mr Parker wanted to check a new arrival.

"Just to make sure she's settling in," he said as he and Neil crossed the courtyard.

"What breed is she?" asked Neil.

"A greyhound," said Bob Parker. "She belongs to Tom Hastings. He's got the garage on the Compton Road."

Neil followed his father into Kennel Block One. There was a row of ten pens on either side with sleeping quarters for each dog and access to an outside run.

"Hey, Bobby!" Neil said as a cairn terrier threw itself at the wire mesh. "How are you?"

Bobby rolled over in ecstasy as Neil opened the door of the pen and tickled him. Then the little dog jumped up and scampered over to the corner where he pounced on a squeaky ball.

"OK," said Neil. "I'll throw it for you."

Bob Parker laughed. "You'll be there all night if Bobby has anything to do with it," he said. "I'll be down at the far end."

Neil threw the ball for Bobby a few times then gave the cairn a pat.

"Gotta go," he said, throwing the ball one last time.

The dogs often had their favourite toys at the kennels. Some even had their own cushions and blankets. It made them feel more at home.

Neil made his way down to the end of the block, stopping to stroke a golden retriever whose owner was in hospital, and to make a fuss of a cocker spaniel who clearly thought that King Street Kennels was the perfect doggy hotel. Caspar had made himself at home from the moment he arrived.

Bob Parker was in the end pen with the greyhound.

"She looks just fine," he said as Neil came into the pen. "Good girl, Tess."

"Wow!" Neil said, staring at the dog. "You didn't tell me she was having puppies, Dad!"

Mr Parker smiled. "It's early days yet,"

he said as he looked at the elegant greyhound. "She's only with us for a few days. Tom had to go to a sales conference – and the organizers didn't fancy a pregnant greyhound on the premises."

Neil bent down and stroked the greyhound's sleek coat. Tess gazed up at him with liquid eyes.

"You're going to have such gorgeous puppies," Neil said.

Mr Parker smiled. "She certainly should," he said. "She's a real beauty. She's already bred some winners."

"You mean her puppies will be racing greyhounds?" asked Neil.

"They've got the pedigree for it," Mr Parker said. "But we must be sure to take extra-special care of this little lady."

"Oh, we will," said Neil. Then his face clouded as he remembered the bobtail.

He told his dad all about it as they checked the remaining pens and locked up. Then they made their way to the barn where Mr Parker would be taking the regular Wednesday night obedience class. Sam came rushing out to meet them.

"Tied up?" said Mr Parker as Neil finished his story. "But you said the dog wasn't ill-treated."

"Well, he didn't much like being tied up," said Neil. "But he seemed all right apart from that." He looked down at Sam. "Can you imagine tying Sam up like that? His owner must be really mean."

"Now don't go jumping to conclusions," Mr Parker said. "There might be a good reason. The dog might be dangerous."

"No way," said Neil firmly. "He was as soft as they come."

Mr Parker rumpled his dark brown hair.

"I don't think the dog belongs to Mr Taylor," he said. "I was talking to him a few weeks ago. I'm sure he'd have mentioned it if he was getting a dog."

"So what am I going to do?" asked Neil.

His father put his arm round Neil's shoulder as they stopped at the barn door.

"Look," he said. "Leave it with me. I'll make some enquiries in the morning. If there's a dog being maltreated, we'll find out."

"And do something about it?" said Neil.

"You bet," said Mr Parker. "Now come and see Sandy. Alex Harvey is bringing him and Finn to the obedience class tonight."

"Sandy!" said Neil. "I haven't seen him for ages."

Neil felt a lot better now that he had shared his problem with his dad. That was the great thing about his parents. They knew exactly how he felt about dogs.

As they entered the barn a sandy-coloured mongrel lolloped across the floor, wagging his tail.

"Sandy!" said Neil, bending down to pat him.

Sandy had been brought to the rescue centre in a very bad way. He had been so badly treated he didn't trust anybody. But Neil had made the dog his special project and won him round with patience and lots of attention. Once Sandy had stopped being afraid of everyone, he had turned out to be the best-natured dog in the world.

"How do you think he's looking?" Alex Harvey said, coming over to them.

Neil looked up. Alex Harvey was a doctor in Compton. He was a large, untidy man with a shock of red hair and a beard. He had adopted Sandy.

Mr Parker had thought of offering Sandy for adoption to a young family in Padsham but when Dr Harvey saw him it was love at first sight.

"He looks terrific," Neil said, looking at the mongrel's shining coat and bright eyes. "I'm really glad you took him on."

Alex Harvey smiled. "I couldn't believe it the first time I saw Sandy," he said. "He reminded me of Rory, a dog I used to have when I was your age. How could I resist him?"

"Are he and Finn getting on OK?" asked Neil.

Alex Harvey ran a hand through his hair. "They were to begin with," he said. "Sandy's a really good-natured dog. He was quite timid with Finn at first, but he's gained a lot in confidence lately – and now I think Finn's getting a little jealous. He's been acting up a bit recently."

"He'll be trying to get your attention again," said Neil. "It must be difficult for him with a new dog in the house. He probably just wants to show you and Sandy that *he's* still top dog."

"I just hope it works out," said Alex Harvey. "I couldn't give Sandy up – not now. It would be like losing Rory all over again."

"It'll work out," said Neil. "Finn probably still needs time to get used to Sandy."

"I'm sure you're right," Alex Harvey said. "I *hope* you are."

"Where *is* Finn?" asked Neil.

Dr Harvey pointed over towards the back of the barn. Carole Parker was putting the terrier through his paces. Finn was a pedigree Kerry blue – a showdog and a prizewinner.

"He's looking beautiful," Neil said. "Are you entering him in the Manchester show?"

"I want to," said Dr Harvey. "But we've got to sort out those little problems first."

Neil nodded. Kerry blues were lovely dogs with wavy silky blue coats and long rectangular heads. But they were also very independent and could be extremely boisterous.

"He's keeping well to heel at the

moment," Mr Parker said, looking at the dog.

Dr Harvey nodded. "That's your doing," he said. "He wouldn't do that for me!"

Mr Parker laughed. "We'll get him calmed down for the show," he said. "He needs to know he's still just as important to you as he ever was." He looked down at Sandy. "Have you tried training him with Sandy?"

Dr Harvey looked surprised. "No," he said. "Sandy doesn't need obedience training."

Mr Parker nodded. "That's just the point," he said. "Sometimes a pedigree dog will train much better with a calmer-natured dog – especially a mongrel like Sandy."

"Who are you calling a mongrel?" Neil said in a huff. "Sandy's a cross-breed."

"A cross-breed of quite a lot of dogs," his father said, laughing. "But he's got a wonderfully calm nature. Let's give it a try. If Finn sees Sandy getting praise, he'll want praise too and maybe he'll behave."

Neil watched as Dr Harvey went off with

21

his dad and the two dogs. Bob Parker handed over the leads to Dr Harvey and asked him to walk the dogs at heel. At first Finn was very frisky but Sandy stayed perfectly calm, listening intently to the commands, obeying immediately. Alex Harvey praised him with a pat for every command obeyed. Gradually Finn began to calm down and Alex was able to give him praise too.

"That's amazing," said Neil.

"It's a good trick," said Mr Parker. "Pedigree dogs are often highly strung and Kerry blues are very strong-minded. You need to keep up the training with them."

"Isn't Sandy great?" said Neil.

"He's no showdog, but he's a fine . . . cross-breed," Mr Parker finished.

Neil grinned. "I'm going to take Sam round the Agility course before it gets dark," he said. "He's been doing really well lately."

Mr Parker nodded. "He's a sheepdog," he said. "Sheepdogs are very intelligent animals. And they've got great memories. He's perfect for Agility training."

"I thought I'd add a new obstacle tonight," said Neil.

"Why don't you get Emily to help you? I'll see you after the lesson."

Bob Parker strode over to where his class was waiting for him. The dogs were mostly new owners with very excitable puppies. Neil knew that in a few weeks they would be sitting on command, coming when called and walking at heel – just like all the dogs that came to King Street for obedience training.

Neil found Emily outside with Sarah and they made their way to the kennel store where they kept their equipment.

"I'll help too," Sarah said. "Do you think I could train Fudge to go over the course?"

"Not tonight," Neil said firmly. "We've still got a lot to do with Sam. I want to try putting a set of steps at the end of the see-saw this time. There should be a stepladder in the store."

"Have you been thinking about the Agility competition at the Manchester show?" said Emily.

Neil nodded. "Yeah, I'd love to enter Sam," he said. "But I want to make sure he's in top form. That's why I want to try this new obstacle. I don't know if he'll be ready in time."

"If we plan out a regular programme of training we could do it," Emily said.

"Will you help?" Neil asked.

"Of course I will," said Emily. "So will Steve."

Steve Tansley was the Parkers' cousin. He lived in Compton. He had a golden Labrador called Ricky who Mr Parker reckoned was as near untrainable as a dog could get.

"I don't see any steps," said Emily, looking round the store.

"What a pain," Neil said. "I wonder where they are."

"What about tea chests?" Sarah said. "There are loads of them in here."

"That's a good idea," Emily said. "We can pile them up – like a sort of mountain."

"Like a pyramid," said Sarah.

"OK," Neil said. "It's worth a try."

Emily and Sarah helped Neil haul everything out. It took them quite a few trips to the field but eventually they had a sort of pyramid of tea chests set up at the far end of the see-saw.

Neil looked at the course. There was a long tube that Sam had to wriggle down, then a tyre hanging from a frame that he had to leap through, then came a plank walkway between two bricks, and a line of posts that he had to weave in and out of. The see-saw was a plank of wood balanced on bricks, and now there were the steps made from piled-up boxes.

Sam would have to negotiate the see-saw then spring onto the first of the steps, climb to the top and back down the other side.

Sarah dusted off her hands. "There now," she said. "Go on, Sam. Do your stuff."

Neil led Sam to the start of the course and unclipped his lead. "Come on, boy," he said. "Go for it!"

Emily and Sarah watched as Neil ran round the course with Sam, urging him on through the tube, encouraging him to leap for the tyre.

"He's doing great!" Neil shouted as Sam sped along the walkway and wove in and out of the posts. "I'm sure it's the best time yet."

Sarah jumped up and down at the far end of the course. "Come on, Sam," she yelled. "The see-saw now!"

Neil swallowed hard as Sam stepped onto the see-saw. This was always the hardest part for him. Sam didn't like the see-saw.

Sarah clapped her hands in excitement

as Sam balanced at the middle of the plank and began the descent. It was perfect.

"Well done, Sam!" she yelled, flinging her arms wide just as Neil urged Sam onto the first step of the pyramid.

The collie looked at the pile of tea chests suspiciously. As his front paw touched the first step, Sarah's arm knocked one of the upper tea chests. The pyramid wobbled and Neil looked on in horror. Sam's back legs skidded on the see-saw as the tea chests teetered above him. Then the whole pyramid came crashing down. Sam yelped as a flying tea chest caught him on the flank.

"Sam!" Neil yelled, making a dive for him.

But Sam was buried under the pile of tea chests.

"Help me," Neil shouted, pulling at the tea chests. There was a furious barking as Sam leapt out and stood growling.

"Oh no," said Neil. "Look!"

Sam was standing in front of the see-saw and the tea chests, his hackles up. His head was down, growling.

"Quick," said Emily. "Get the things back up. Take him over the course again before he can think too much about it."

But it was no good. Sam wouldn't move. He just stood there, growling softly.

Neil's shoulders slumped and he dug his hands deep into his pockets. He felt utterly dejected.

"After all our hard work," he said, his voice heavy with disappointment. "It's all wasted. Sam won't trust that course again – or any Agility course. Now I'll never be able to enter him in a competition."

Emily and Sarah looked at him. "We can try again," said Emily. "We can train him again."

Neil shook his head. "You know what Dad says about sheepdogs," he replied. "They've got good memories. Sam isn't going to forget this."

Chapter Three

Neil and Chris looked for the Old English sheepdog on the way to school next morning.

"He's *still* tied up," Neil said, peering over the garden hedge. "I don't believe anybody could be so cruel. Listen to him."

The big sheepdog was chewing on the rope. He looked up when he heard the boys' voices and gave a low bark. Then he howled again.

Chris shook his head. "He sounds even more miserable than yesterday," he said. "But what can we do?"

Neil's mouth set in a grim line. "I

promised Dad I wouldn't do anything," he said. "At any rate, not yet. Dad is going to try and find out what's going on. He doesn't think it's Mr Taylor's dog."

"We'd better get on then," said Chris.

"Wait a minute," Neil said, digging his hand into his pocket.

"But we'll be late for school," Chris said. "And you know what Smiler's like if you're late. A five-minute lecture at the very least."

Smiler was Mr Hamley, Neil's teacher. He was a good teacher but very strict about timekeeping.

Neil brought out a handful of dog treats and held them out to the bobtail. The big shaggy dog lumbered over to the gate, stretching the rope as far as it would go.

"Look at that," said Neil as the bobtail wolfed down the biscuits. "Do you think he's hungry?"

Chris shook his head. "I don't know about that," he said. "I've never seen a dog refuse a biscuit, have you?"

Neil smiled in spite of himself. That was true enough. Maybe he *was* getting things out of proportion. After all, the dog didn't seem badly treated apart from being tied up.

"OK," he said to Chris. "Let's go. But we're coming home this way just to see if he's still tied up."

"Right," said Chris. "Only come on!"

Assembly had started when Neil and Chris arrived and they got a long look from Mr Hamley.

"You like to live dangerously, don't you?" Hasheem said to them as they shuffled into line beside him at the back of the school hall.

Neil grinned. Hasheem was the class joker. He always made Neil feel better.

"Living on the edge – that's us," he said.

"Tell that to Smiler," Hasheem said.

Neil looked at the stage at the front of the school hall where the teachers were gathered. The window behind them was wide open despite the chilly weather. The headmaster was a fresh air fiend. Mr Hamley was looking straight at Neil. Neil decided to avoid his gaze and concentrate on listening to the announcements.

"Football fixtures for the term," the headmaster said. "The teams are up on the noticeboard."

Chris was immediately all ears. In fact he and Neil were both so attentive to the news that they hardly noticed the noise at first.

"What's that?" said Hasheem.

Pupils began to turn round, muttering and wondering where the noise was coming from.

"It's a dog," Neil said. Then he stopped. "I recognize that bark," he said.

That was as far as he got. The next moment there was a crash as a huge furry grey bundle threw itself through the open window at the end of the room.

"Uh-oh!" said Chris as a row of pot plants went flying. "Do I know that dog or do I know that dog?"

The furry grey bundle skidded to a halt and there, on the stage, looking around the hall, was the Old English sheepdog!

"He got free," said Neil. "He must have chewed through the rope."

"What are you talking about?" Hasheem said.

The bobtail leapt off the stage and lolloped across the hall, barking his head off and looking like an outsize animated floor mop.

"Somebody catch that dog!" the headmaster shouted, leaping down from the stage.

Mr Hamley wasn't far behind him.

Some pupils at the front of the hall squealed in mingled delight and fear while others tried to catch the dog. But the sheepdog was just too big and heavy for them to hold.

Emily was down at the front. She took off after the dog.

"I've got him!" she yelled, hanging on to his collar as the bobtail dragged her sliding across the floor.

"Ow!" yelled another girl. "He trod on my toe."

Neil and Chris were on their way, pushing through the crowd to get to the front.

"We'll get him," Neil yelled.

Then he stopped. He saw a fair-haired girl move towards the dog. The dog turned and gave a great howl – this time of delight – and threw himself at the girl. The girl disappeared from view as the dog leapt, his great hairy paws flat on her chest.

Neil yelled at the dog. "Down, boy!" using his very best obedience training voice.

The dog looked up, howled, and charged straight for him. People got out of the way – fast.

"Keep calm! Stay still!" the headmaster shouted as chairs overturned and pupils went flying in all directions.

"Look out, Neil!" Chris said just as the bobtail launched himself.

Neil went down like a stone and lay there, gazing up at the Bobtail's furry face while the dog started to lick him.

"Down, boy," he said weakly.

Emily and the fair-haired girl arrived and stood over Neil. The girl looked at the dog.

"Ben!" she said. "Get off!"

The bobtail looked up, gave Neil a last lick, and got off. He sat down on the girl's feet and looked up at her adoringly.

"Oh, Ben!" she said. "You're such a bad boy. Now look what you've done."

"Are you all right, Julie?" Emily said.

Neil looked at the girl. Julie! This must be Julie Baker, the moaning Minnie. And Ben was her *dog*, not her brother!

"Ben's a dog?" he said. "Ben's *your* dog?"

Julie smiled. "Sorry," she said. "I can't think why he picked on you."

Neil stood up, dusting himself down. "It's

35

OK," he said. "We've met already, Ben and I."

Julie looked surprised. "But he hasn't been out of the garden since we arrived – only for walks with me on the playing fields."

"I saw him in the garden – tied up!" Neil said.

Julie flushed. "Oh, he wasn't very happy, was he?"

"Not very," said Neil grimly.

"I can explain," said Julie.

But she didn't get a chance.

"Watch out!" said Chris. "Here comes Smiler."

"Now I've got you into trouble," Julie said to Neil.

Hasheem put his head on one side. "Oh, don't worry about that," he said. "Neil likes living on the edge."

Neil groaned and Chris tried to disappear into the crowd. Mr Hamley forced himself through the ranks of pupils all trying to pat the dog.

"Well, well," he said. "I might have known you would be at the bottom of this,

Neil Parker. You're never far away when there's a dog around."

Neil's heart sank. Late for assembly and now this. He was sure to get detention.

Chapter Four

"T hat wasn't so bad," Emily said as the three of them walked across the playing fields towards Jarvis Road.

"Yeah, thanks for explaining, Julie," Neil said.

Julie smiled. "Don't mention it," she said. "You were really good about Ben flattening you like that. He only does it to people he likes."

Neil laughed. "I'm glad he likes me," he said. "But I wish he had another way of showing it."

"I reckon the headmaster was pleased

when we offered to take Ben home," Emily said.

"I think he was just glad to see the back of him," Julie said. "Ben did make a terrible mess of the school hall."

"Is that why you keep him tied up?" Neil asked.

Julie flushed at the criticism in his tone. "No," she said. "We're used to Ben. We don't mind him bumping into things and making a mess. It's just that Mum is in the house on her own. We only moved in at the weekend and Dad is working in Saudi Arabia. He won't be home for ages yet."

"But why tie him up?" said Emily.

"It's for his own safety," Julie said. "At the moment, Mum's having the house done up, so there are workmen all over the place – and Ben loves making friends."

"We noticed," Neil said.

"He hates not knowing what's going on," Julie said. "The workmen are hauling out the old bathroom suite and putting in a new kitchen. It could be dangerous for Ben. There are floorboards up and electric wires everywhere. Ben is so curious – and he likes to 'help'."

"Oh," said Neil. "I suppose that's different. It's just that he sounded so miserable."

Julie nodded. "That's because he's never been tied up before," she said. "He couldn't understand what was going on."

"Tying him up didn't seem to work," Emily said.

Julie grinned. "I don't know what we're going to do with him," she said. "The workmen will be around for another few days."

Neil looked at her. He was getting an idea, but maybe he'd better talk to his parents first.

"So you've moved into Mr Taylor's house," said Emily. "We didn't know Mr Taylor had moved out permanently."

"He's gone to live with his daughter in Manchester," Julie said. "Mum bought the house from him. It was all done in a bit of a rush and the house needs a lot of work."

"You didn't have much time to get used to the idea of moving, then?" Neil said.

Julie shrugged. "I'll get used to it," she

said. "It's just that I had to leave all my friends behind. And Ben was happy there, too. There were meadows nearby where he could get a good run. He used to love running through the fields." She dug a hand into her blazer pocket and pulled out a photograph. "Look!" she said. "I always keep this with me."

Neil and Emily looked at the photo. It was Ben, romping through a field full of long grass and poppies.

"He looks really happy," said Emily. "I can see how he would miss it."

"He does," said Julie. "I don't think he understands what's happened. He tries to follow me everywhere."

"He certainly managed to follow you today," Neil said. "He must be a bloodhound in disguise."

Julie laughed. "I've taken him over the playing fields a few times for walks," she said. "He would expect to find me around there somewhere. He probably heard noises from the school hall."

"Clever dog," said Emily.

"He's a sheepdog," Julie said. "It's in his

blood. Dogs like Ben were bred to look after sheep, find them in the snow, that kind of thing. It's instinctive."

"You know a lot about dogs, then," Neil said.

Julie shrugged. "Not really," she said. "But I know Ben."

Neil watched Julie as she bent to ruffle the fur at Ben's neck. And to think he had imagined that Ben's owner didn't care for him. Julie *loved* Ben.

"You'll like living here," he said to Julie. "Especially when you make friends."

"Oh, she's made friends already," Emily said.

Julie looked surprised. "Who?"

Emily grinned. "Us, of course," she said. "And don't worry about Ben, either. We'll introduce him to *lots* of doggy friends."

"Our parents run King Street Kennels just up the road," Neil said. "There are always loads of dogs around at home. We've got a dog of our own."

"What kind?" said Julie, interested.

"A Border collie," Neil said. He smiled. "He's a sheepdog too, like Ben."

"But not quite so big," Emily said as Ben tried to pull away from her.

"Here we are," Julie said, turning in at the back gate of her house.

A blonde-haired woman in dusty jeans came hurrying out of the back door.

"Oh, there he is," said Mrs Baker. "Thank goodness you found him. I was just about to go out looking."

Ben lurched towards her but Julie held on to his collar with both hands. "Oh no you don't," she said. She looked at her mother. "What are we going to do with him, Mum? We can't tie him up again."

"You certainly can't," said a voice from the next garden. "That noise was terrible. It gave poor Sheba such a fright."

"Hello, Mrs Fitzherbert," Neil said.

Mrs Fitzherbert sniffed. She was a tall woman with tight grey curls and a thin nose. Sheba, her grey toy poodle, was cradled in her arms. The poor animal was shivering.

"And just what are you doing out of school at this time of the day?" she said to Neil. "And your sister, too."

"We've got permission," Emily said. "We were bringing Ben back. He escaped from the garden."

"Now I suppose you're going to tie him up again," said Mrs Fitzherbert. "Great hulking beast! If I hear that dog howling just once more I'll report it to the police. Sheba is very highly strung and delicate. She can't stand that kind of noise. And she has a big competition coming up – she's sure to win a prize this time if she's at her best and not upset. I'll have you know that both Sheba's parents were prizewinners and Sheba is a perfect specimen of her breed. But she doesn't like noisy, nasty, big dogs."

"Dad saw Sheba at a show once," Neil said softly.

Mrs Fitzherbert was still ranting on to Julie's mother.

"Did she win a prize?" Julie whispered.

Neil shook his head. "Dad said she was far too nervous of the other dogs."

"No wonder," Emily said. "Mrs Fitz doesn't let any other dogs near her. She isn't used to them. Somebody should tell Mrs Fitz it takes more than just breeding to win prizes."

"Are you volunteering?" said Neil.

"No way," said Emily.

Mrs Fitzherbert had come to the end of her tirade.

"I want that dog kept quiet," she said.

"It's so difficult," Julie's mother said. "I've got workmen in the house. Things are a bit of a mess."

"So I see," said Mrs Fitzherbert, looking at Mrs Baker's dusty jeans. "But I've said the last word on the subject. Either you stop that dog howling or I report it to the police. I won't stand for it and that's flat!"

Mrs Fitzherbert turned on her heel and marched off into her house.

"Huh!" said Julie. "Delicate! That's a laugh. I caught Sheba snarling through the fence at Ben, and when he went over to make friends she nipped his nose."

"Oh, dear," said Mrs Baker. "We haven't got off to a very good start with our neighbour, have we?"

Julie snorted. "Nobody could," she said. "She has fits every time she sees Ben."

"Oh, Ben," Mrs Baker said. "What are we going to do with you?"

Neil decided he'd better not wait to ask his parents about his idea.

"Look, Mrs Baker," he said. "It's only a problem during the day, isn't it?"

Mrs Baker nodded. "Once Julie comes home from school, one of us can always keep an eye on him and make sure he stays out of mischief," she said.

"Our parents run a boarding kennels," Neil said. "Maybe Ben could spend the day-time there."

"Brilliant!" said Emily.

"He would miss Julie wherever he was," Neil went on. "But at least he wouldn't have to be tied up. And he would have other dogs for company."

"It would only be for two or three days," Mrs Baker said. "What do you think, Julie?"

Julie beamed. "I think it's a great idea," she said.

"If I could phone Dad, maybe you could take Ben over to the kennels this afternoon," Neil said.

"That would be marvellous," Mrs Baker replied.

She led the way into the house and showed Neil the phone.

"Oh, Neil," said Bob Parker when Neil got through, "I found out who that bobtail belongs to."

Neil grinned. "So did I," he replied. "In fact, that's why I'm phoning."

It didn't take Neil long to fix things up with his dad. He put the phone down and turned to the Bakers.

"That's OK," he said. "You can take Ben

over any time. Then you can come over after tea and collect him."

"What a relief," Julie said to her mother. "I hated having to tie Ben up, and Neil likes Ben already."

"So do I," said Emily. "And so will Mum and Dad – and Sarah, and Sam and Fudge and Kate."

Julie looked puzzled.

"Come on," said Neil. "We'd better get back to school. We'll explain on the way."

Emily did most of the talking. Julie had got the entire family history by the time they got back to school. Neil's mind was on something else. Mrs Fitzherbert had reminded him about Sam and the Manchester dog show. She must be entering Sheba in it. He sighed. Would he even be able to get Sam to take part in the show?

Chapter Five

"**A**ren't you going to train Sam to-night?" Sarah asked Neil after tea that evening. They were in the courtyard outside the kennels with Sam and Ben.

"I tried but it was no good," Neil said, looking down at Sam. "He won't go near the course."

Emily looked at Sam. "Poor Sam," she said. "He got such a fright."

They turned at the sound of bicycle wheels, scrunching on the gravel.

"There's Steve," Sarah shouted, running to meet him. Sarah really liked her big cousin.

"Hi, munchkin!" Steve said to her, parking his bike. Then he saw Ben. "Hey! What a beauty. Where did you get him?"

Neil laughed and explained.

"Julie and her mum are coming over later to collect him," Emily said.

"So where's the Agility course?" Steve said. "I thought Sam was in training."

Sam wagged his tail at the sound of his name and Steve scratched him under the chin.

"He won't go near it," Neil said, dejectedly. "Some tea chests toppled over last night and gave him a scare. I feel terrible about it."

"We don't have to use the tea chests," said Emily. "We don't even have to use the see-saw for the moment. We can start with the basics again. It might work – it's worth a try, at least."

"I agree," said Steve. "And, look! I've done a plan of the course on my new colour printer. We can try out new designs without having to heave all the stuff around."

Steve was a computer whizz. He was always thinking up things to do on his PC.

Neil looked at the sheet Steve handed him. The course was marked out with distances between the obstacles listed and spaces for times in a column down the side.

"You see," said Steve, "we list Sam's time for each part of the course against the distances. If we do that over a few trial runs we can get an idea where his weak spots are. It's a training programme."

"Can you do one for Fudge?" Sarah asked.

Steve laughed. "Of course I can," he said. "I'll do a wheel for him and you can time how long it takes him to go round ten times."

"Brilliant!" said Sarah.

"This looks great," Neil said, examining the training plan. He looked at Emily. "Maybe we *can* try again," he said.

Emily was already looking at Steve's plan. "According to this, we need a barrel."

"There's one in the kennel store," Neil said. "I'll get it."

Julie and her mum arrived just as they got the course set up – without the see-saw and boxes but *with* the barrel.

"Hi! Over here!" Neil yelled as they drew up in the driveway.

Ben hurled himself at them, clearing the field fence in one leap. Julie gave him a hug as he planted his huge paws on her chest. Sam scampered over to the action.

"This must be Sam," Julie said when she got her breath back. "He's beautiful." Then she looked at the course laid out in the field. "What's that?"

"An Agility course," Emily said as Steve and Neil showed Julie the plan.

"I'll just go in and see your parents," Mrs Baker said. "I won't be long."

Emily was watching Sam and Ben. "Oh, don't rush – please," she said to Mrs Baker. "Just look at Sam and Ben."

The two dogs snuffled at each other, then Sam put out a paw and pushed Ben on the flank. Ben gave a short bark and circled Sam.

"They're playing," said Neil. "They like each other."

"They're both sheepdogs," Julie said. "Of course they like each other." She looked at the Agility course. "Do you think Ben could ever do anything like that?"

Steve burst out laughing. "I don't think the tyres are big enough for him to get through," he said.

"Or the barrel," Emily said. "But he could probably walk the plank and wriggle through the tube. Why don't you let him have a go?"

"Can I?" Julie said. "Will you show me how?"

Neil clipped Sam's lead on and led him towards the plank. "Come on, Sam," he said gently. "Show Julie how clever you are."

But Sam backed off, growling low in his throat.

"It's no good," said Neil. "He won't go near it even without the tea chests."

Emily explained Sam's problem to Julie.

"That's such a shame," Julie said. Then she looked round. "Ben!"

Ben had started off along the plank. His great paws covered it almost entirely as he padded towards the barrel at the other end.

"Uh-oh!" said Steve. "He's going to try and go through the barrel."

"He'll never make it," said Julie. "He's too big. I'll get him."

But Neil stopped her. "No!" he said softly. "Leave him. Look at Sam!"

They all looked. The collie was nosing the end of the plank, looking at Ben padding along it. With a fluid leap, he sprang onto the walkway and stepped gracefully along the length of it. Ben, great lumbering Ben, turned and the plank wobbled.

Neil held his breath but Sam didn't flinch. Very gently he prodded Ben in the rear with his nose and the bobtail flopped off onto the ground. Sam looked at him as if to say "This is my territory", then he was off round the course, sliding through the barrel like a shadow, skimming through the tyre and weaving his way through the posts.

"Wow!" said Neil. "He's doing it!"

"He wouldn't let Ben get the better of him," Emily said, laughing. Then she squealed. "Oh, no!"

Before they could stop him, Ben made a leap for the barrel. He got halfway through, his front paws at one end and his back paws at the other.

"He's stuck," Julie said and moved towards him. But Ben was moving again, lumbering after Sam, a barrel on legs. Steve, Neil, Julie and Emily chased after him. Sarah was doubled up with laughter. Ben wasn't able to move very fast but they were all laughing so much it was a while before they caught up with him. Sam took no notice, finished the course and sat waiting for praise.

"Got him!" Julie said, grabbing Ben. "But how do we get him out of the barrel?"

"With great difficulty," said Neil, patting Sam. "I don't think we've ever had this problem before."

"A first for King Street Kennels," Emily said as she and Julie hauled on the barrel while Steve and Neil hauled on Ben.

"Never again," Neil said as Ben scrabbled out of the barrel. "No Agility course for you, Ben."

"That isn't fair," said Emily. "After all, if it hadn't been for Ben, Sam wouldn't have tried the course again."

Neil nodded. "You're right," he said. "I'm sorry, Ben. I'll make it up to you."

Julie's mum came out of the house. "Time to go, Julie," she called.

Julie looked disappointed.

"You can come again tomorrow," Emily said. "And all weekend if you like."

"I've got to paint my bedroom," Julie said. "I was really looking forward to doing that, but King Street Kennels is much more fun."

"Why don't we help you paint?" Neil said. "After all, we owe you and Ben a favour."

"Really?" said Julie, her face lighting up. "Great!"

"You can do it on Saturday," Mrs Baker said. "Mrs Fitzherbert is going to visit her niece so you can make as much noise as you want."

"It's a date," said Emily. "How about you, Steve?"

"Count me out," Steve said. "I'm playing football."

Neil glanced round as Ben scrambled into Mrs Baker's car. He took up the whole of the back seat.

"Thanks, Ben," he whispered. "Thanks a lot!"

Chapter Six

By the time Neil and Emily arrived at Julie's house on Saturday all the workmen had gone.

"The house looks great," Emily said.

Mrs Baker smiled. "I'm really glad it's all finished," she replied. "No more trailing wires or holes in the floor."

"We can let Ben have the run of the house again," Julie said. She looked at Neil. "Where's Sam?"

"We thought we'd better leave him at home," Neil replied. "Two dogs around wet paint would be too much to cope with."

"You're probably right," said Julie. "But

Ben will miss him. They're really good friends. Ben loves watching Sam on the Agility course."

Neil nodded. The previous day, Ben and Sam had got on really well. And, now that Ben was content to watch Sam going over the Agility course without joining in, Sam's training had become very successful.

"Sam really showed off for Ben," Emily said. "Every time he finished the course he looked round to see if Ben was watching."

Mrs Baker laughed. "I'm off shopping," she said. "I need to choose a new stair carpet. And I must look for curtains for the dining room. Now, where did I put that scrap of wallpaper? It was just the right shade of green."

"It's on the kitchen counter, Mum," Julie said. "It's beside your list of things to do." She turned to Neil and Emily. "Right, let's get on."

Mrs Baker disappeared into the kitchen muttering to herself.

"What are we going to do with Ben?" Emily asked.

"He can have free run of the house and

garden – except for my bedroom," Julie said. "We don't want him getting anywhere near wet paint."

Mrs Baker came out of the kitchen clutching the piece of wallpaper and her list. "Oh, dear," she said, looking at the list. "I forgot to ask the builders about getting the fence mended. It's really rickety and Mrs Fitzherbert's been dropping hints about it."

"It's her fence too," said Julie.

"Not according to Mrs Fitzherbert," Mrs Baker said. "She says it's our responsibility. I'll get somebody to have a look at it on Monday."

"Good idea, Mum," Julie said. "Stop worrying and enjoy your shopping."

"Carpet, curtains – oh, and curtain poles." Mrs Baker looked at the list in her hand. "See you later, you three. Be good."

"Finished," Julie said, wiping a hand across her forehead and leaving a streak of white paint.

"It's great," said Neil, looking round Julie's bedroom.

The carpet wasn't down yet and the windows were still bare but the room looked terrific. They had painted the walls white and the woodwork a deep blue.

"Just wait till I get my posters up," said Julie. "It'll be brilliant. Thanks a lot, you two. It would have taken me ages to do this on my own."

"We should set up in business," Emily said.

"No way," said Neil. "The only business I want to be in is the dog business."

Julie frowned. "That reminds me. Where's Ben?"

Emily looked out of the window. "He isn't in the garden," she said.

"He must be in the house somewhere," Neil said, opening the bedroom door.

There was a rush of grey-blue fur as Ben lolloped into the room and began to lick Julie's hand.

"He must have been waiting quietly outside the door all this time," Julie said. "Oh, Ben, what a good boy you are!"

Ben barked and put a paw on Julie's chest.

"Down," said Julie.

Ben dropped to all fours and looked at her soulfully.

"Oh, all right," Julie said, opening her arms. "Come on, softie!"

Ben reared up and planted his paws on her chest.

"The paint!" said Emily as Julie staggered back.

But it was too late. Ben's back paw knocked over a pot of white paint. It trickled round his paw and he dropped back down

to investigate, dipping his front paws into it.

"No, Ben!" Neil said.

Ben looked at them, dabbled his nose in the paint, sneezed and lumbered out of the room and down the stairs.

Neil, Julie and Emily dashed after him.

"Oh, look at his pawprints!" Julie cried as Ben left a trail of white prints on the floorboards behind him. "Thank goodness Mum hasn't had any of the carpets laid yet."

They followed the trail of white pawprints down the stairs and into the garden.

"Ben, you naughty boy," Julie said.

Ben barked and took off round the garden.

"Keep him here," said Neil. "I'll get a basin of water and some shampoo."

"Make it a big basin," Emily yelled as she and Julie set off after Ben.

They collared him just as Neil staggered out of the house with the biggest basin he could, find full of soapy water.

"Front paws first," he said.

Julie and Emily grabbed a paw each and

planted them firmly in the basin. But it wasn't easy keeping the rest of Ben out of the water. Neil scrubbed away at his paws and nose while Ben struggled against them.

"Ow!" said Julie as flying drops of water caught her in the eye. She put her hands up to her eyes. "Stop it, Ben. I've already had one shower today."

There was the sound of a car driving up next door and Emily looked round, letting go of Ben.

"Watch out!" said Neil. "Ben's off!"

"It's Mrs Fitz," said Emily, looking at the car.

Julie made a grab for Ben but she was too late. He had seen Mrs Fitzherbert get out of the car with Sheba in her arms – and he was determined to make friends.

He hurled himself at the fence and put his front paws up on it. Neil, Emily and Julie watched in horror as the fence sagged and then gave way entirely. Ben stepped over it and plodded up to Mrs Fitzherbert.

Sheba yapped and Mrs Fitzherbert turned round.

"Go away!" she yelled at Ben. "You're all wet!"

Ben started to shake himself vigorously. Drops of water flew in all directions – but mostly they landed on Mrs Fitzherbert and Sheba.

Mrs Fitzherbert raised a hand to her face and Sheba leapt out of her arms. The little dog bared her teeth and stood facing Ben.

It was an amazing sight – the tiny toy poodle, beautifully clipped, and the enormous shaggy sheepdog. But it was Ben who backed off as the little dog snapped and yapped at him.

"You nasty animal!" Mrs Fitzherbert shouted at Ben. "And you nasty child!" she said to Julie. "I told your mother to get that fence fixed. Just look at poor Sheba."

Neil was looking at Sheba. The little dog was shaking. She looked very nervous. But still she stood her ground and made Ben back down. She was a brave little thing.

"Your mother will hear about this," Mrs Fitzherbert said as she scooped Sheba up and marched into the house.

"There she goes, having fits again!" said

Julie. "Ben only wanted to be friends. It was Sheba that was snapping. What a horrible spoilt little dog she is."

Neil frowned. He never blamed dogs – only their owners.

"No she isn't," he said. "At least, she might be a bit spoilt but she's got lots of courage, standing up to a great big dog like Ben."

"Ben wouldn't have hurt her," Julie said.

Neil shook his head. "*I* know that and *you* know that," he said. "But Sheba doesn't. She's never been used to other dogs. She doesn't know how to behave with them. Didn't you see how terrified she was?"

"Huh!" said Julie. "That was just bad temper."

Emily looked thoughtful. "You know, I think Neil's right," she said. "If Sheba never mixes with other dogs she's bound to resent them when she meets them."

Neil nodded. "Pedigree dogs often have attitude problems," he said. "They need to mix with other dogs – ordinary dogs, not showdogs."

Julie looked doubtful. "Maybe you *are* right," she said. "You said your dad saw Sheba at a show and she was really nervous of the other dogs."

"It must be just terrifying for her to have to go into a show with all those strange dogs," said Neil. "Can you imagine how frightened she must be?"

Emily nodded. "Poor little thing," she said. "Isn't there anything we can do?"

Neil shook his head. "Do *you* want to try and tell Mrs Fitzherbert how to look after Sheba?" he said.

"No way," said Emily. "But I still feel sorry for Sheba."

Julie bit her lip. "I suppose I do too," she said. "Maybe it's Mrs Fitz I dislike so much, not Sheba."

"I wish there was something we could do," said Emily.

Julie tilted her head to one side, thinking. "You said that dogs like Sheba need ordinary dogs – normal dogs," she said.

Neil nodded. "It seems to calm them down."

"Well, Ben is a normal dog . . ." Julie said

thoughtfully. "So if Ben and Sheba could become friends then Sheba might get over her nervousness."

"But how are they ever going to get the chance?" Emily asked. "It isn't Sheba's fault. Mrs Fitz is the real problem and she won't let Ben near Sheba."

Neil frowned. It didn't really matter who the real problem was – it was Sheba that was suffering and he couldn't stand to see a dog suffer. He sighed. There must be *something* they could do.

Chapter Seven

Tom Hastings, Tess's owner, came to collect the greyhound on Sunday morning. He was a short, thickset man, wearing blue overalls and a baseball cap. Neil was putting Sam through his paces on the Agility course with Steve and Emily. Tom came over to watch.

"He's going well," Tom said, looking at Sam.

"Neil is going to enter him in the Agility event at the Manchester dog show," Steve said.

Tom smiled as Emily bent to give Tess a last cuddle.

69

"I'll see you there," he said.

"You aren't entering Tess, are you?" Emily asked.

"No," said Tom. "She'll have a litter of puppies to look after by that time. She'll be far too busy to enter a show. But I'll be there. I'll look out for Sam." He looked at Tess. "And now I'd better get this little lady home."

Neil gave Tess a final pat. "Good luck with the pups, girl," he said. "You're going to be a great mum." They watched as Tom drove off with Tess.

"There's Dr Harvey with Finn and Sandy," Emily said as a car drew up.

Dr Harvey waved to them as he and the dogs walked towards the barn for the obedience class.

Neil frowned. Finn didn't have such a problem with obedience any longer, but he was still showing signs of being jealous of Sandy and that was making him territorial.

"Do you think Finn will be all right for the show?" Emily asked, following Neil's thoughts.

Neil shrugged. "Dad says he still has a bit of a problem," he said. "It's as if Finn is insisting on showing Sandy who's boss. He won't let Sandy eat until he's finished and if Sandy is lying in front of the fire, Finn just moves him off and takes his place."

"Poor Sandy," said Emily. "I don't suppose he stands up to Finn."

Neil shook his head. "Finn's behaviour is making Sandy timid again. The trouble is, if Finn thinks he can get his own way with Sandy, he's likely to try it with other dogs

– and the show judges won't like that."

"Hey, you two," Steve called. "Watch Sam go!"

Neil and Emily turned as Steve set Sam off on the Agility course.

"Wait for me!" Neil yelled, racing along beside the obstacles.

"Go for it, Sam!" Steve shouted, looking at his stopwatch.

Half an hour later Sam was looking better than he had ever done.

"He's brilliant," Emily said as Sam wove in and out of the posts.

Sam shot through the last tyre and raced across the finish line.

"Wow! That was the best time yet," said Neil.

"And he only dropped a few points on the way round," Emily said.

Neil marked in Sam's time and studied the computer sheets.

"He really is making progress," he said. "This was a great idea, Steve."

Steve grinned. "No problem," he said. "But I've got to go."

"More football practice, no doubt?" Emily asked.

Steve looked at the sky. "So long as it doesn't snow."

"Snow?" said Neil. "It's a bit early for that, isn't it?"

Emily shivered and wrapped her anorak more tightly round her. "It said on the weather forecast this morning there might be."

"So much for global warming," Steve said. "See you! Bye, Sam!"

Sam barked and raced Steve and his bike to the front drive. Steve waved as he disappeared in the direction of Compton.

"It looks as if you've got the makings of a champion there," said a voice.

Neil and Emily turned round.

"Oh, hi, Dr Harvey. Hi, Sandy, Finn!" Neil said.

Emily got down between the dogs and gave each of them a one-armed hug.

"I don't think he's good enough yet to win a prize," Neil said, looking at Sam. "But he's good enough to enter."

"He won't disgrace you," Dr Harvey said.

Neil laughed. "Oh, Sam could never do that," he said. Then he looked at Finn. "How is he?"

Dr Harvey shook his head. "Still a bit of a worry," he said. "Your father suggested leaving him here for a night or two to try and break the bad habits he's picking up. He's really started trying to keep Sandy out of 'his patch'."

"Poor Sandy," Emily said. "He wouldn't say boo to a goose."

"Perhaps that's the trouble," Dr Harvey said. "Maybe Finn needs somebody to stand up to him."

"Like Sheba," Neil said.

"Who?" asked Dr Harvey.

Emily laughed. "A really brave little dog we know," she said. "She's only tiny but she would stand up to a lion."

"Maybe you could introduce Finn to her some time," Dr Harvey said. "Sandy is too easygoing to be a match for Finn."

There was a shout from the house and Sarah came running towards them.

"Julie's on the phone," she said to Neil and Emily. "She sounds really upset. She said something about the police."

Neil and Emily looked at each other.

"Ben!" said Julie.

"Oh no," said Neil as they raced towards the house. "I bet Mrs Fitz has reported him to the police!"

Neil picked up the phone. "Are the police still there?" he asked.

Julie gasped. "No, they've gone now," she said.

"What are they going to do about Ben?" asked Emily, her head close to Neil's as they shared the telephone.

"Nothing," said Julie. "Mrs Fitz tried to make out it was Ben's fault. She said he must have come into her garden and scared Sheba away, but the police started to ask about how valuable Sheba was and whether anybody had been hanging around, watching her."

Neil and Emily looked at each other.

"Wait a minute," Neil said to Julie. "I think maybe we've got hold of the wrong end of the stick. *What* was Ben's fault?"

"I thought you'd heard somehow," Julie

said. "Sheba has disappeared. The police think she's been stolen, but Mrs Fitz thinks Ben got over the broken fence and frightened her and she ran away."

"But that's ridiculous," Emily said. "Sheba isn't frightened of Ben. She'd never run away from him. Look at how she stood up to him yesterday."

"Try telling that to Mrs Fitz," Julie said. "She wants Ben locked up."

Emily bit her lip. "Look, Julie," she said. "We'll come over right away. Sheba *must* have been stolen. Even the police think so. Mrs Fitz can't do a thing to Ben."

"I hope not," said Julie. "Hurry, will you?"

Neil dashed through to the office to tell his mother they were off and fill her in on the situation.

"Poor Julie," Carole Parker said. "Tell her Ben can come here any time if things are too difficult with Mrs Fitzherbert."

Neil nodded and raced outside. Emily was talking to Dr Harvey, who was just getting ready to drive away.

"Emily says you're in a hurry to get into

Compton," Dr Harvey said. "Jump in. I'll take you."

Emily got in beside Dr Harvey, and Neil got in the back. Dr Harvey had an estate car with the boot fenced off for the dogs. Finn was sprawled along the back seat and Sandy was curled up in the boot.

"At the moment it's easier to keep them separate when I'm driving," Dr Harvey said.

Neil slid along the seat and put his hand out to Finn. The dog drew back a little then nuzzled Neil's hand and settled down.

"He seems OK with me back here," Neil said.

"It's only other dogs he has the problem with," Dr Harvey said as he drove off. "I might take you up on that introduction to Sheba after all."

"I wish you could," Emily said. "Sheba's been stolen."

Neil and Emily explained the situation and Dr Harvey shook his head.

"I know Mrs Fitzherbert's dog," he said. "I didn't recognize the name, but I remember her from a show. I doubt she's been stolen."

"You mean she isn't valuable?" asked Emily. "Mrs Fitz thinks she is."

"And the police think so too," said Neil.

"The police don't know Sheba," Dr Harvey said. "She's a very nervous dog. She's got real behaviour problems. She's so uptight she can't stop shaking when she's around other dogs. Sure, she has a great pedigree, but that's only half the story. If a dog has a behaviour problem you can forget prizes – that's what worries me so much at the moment with Finn. Anyway, think about it. There would be no point in stealing her. She's registered with the Kennel Club so she couldn't be shown or sold without being identified."

"What about breeding from her?" Neil said. "She could be stolen for that."

Dr Harvey shook his head. "Not with her temperament," he said. "Nobody would want to breed from such a nervous animal. I reckon the police are on the wrong track there. I think she's run off."

"Do you think Ben really did frighten her, then?" Julie said when they reported what Dr Harvey thought.

"No way!" said Emily.

"Mrs Fitz probably left the gate open and Sheba wandered off," Neil said. "You know she's never allowed out of the garden. She's been so protected she would probably get lost quite easily out on her own."

"She won't know anything about crossing roads," said Emily. "What if she's been knocked down? What if she's lying injured somewhere? We have to do something."

"Mrs Fitz is out looking for her," Julie said.

"We could look too," said Neil. "Which way did Mrs Fitz go?"

"She was going to start at the main road," Julie said. "She's worried Sheba might get run over."

"OK," said Neil. "There's no point in covering the same ground. Let's search down by the river."

"Can we take Ben?" Julie said. "I don't want to leave him here in case Mrs Fitz comes back."

"Sure," said Emily. "He might be a help."

But although they searched for nearly

an hour there was no trace of Sheba.

"It's getting really cold," Julie said, pulling her anorak hood up. She looked up at the sky. "Look at those clouds."

Neil looked. The sky was heavy with yellow-grey snow clouds. His heart sank.

"If it snows, that poor little dog won't stand a chance," he said. "She's clipped. She doesn't have any coat to keep her warm."

Visions of Sheba lying shivering and injured filled their minds. Neil looked at the lead-coloured river. "I'm beginning to hope she *has* been stolen," he said. "At least she'd be safe."

Suddenly Ben started barking and pulling at his lead.

"What is it, boy?" Julie said. "Have you scented something? Is it Sheba?"

Ben lifted his head and barked again. The sound boomed across the river. There was a flurry of movement from a belt of trees overhanging the water and Mrs Fitzherbert appeared.

"Oh, it's only Mrs Fitz," Julie said, disappointed.

Ben continued to pull at his lead but Julie held him back.

"No, Ben," she said. "You're in enough trouble with her already."

"What are you doing here?" Mrs Fitzherbert said, coming up to them. "And what are you doing with that brute of a dog? He should be locked up after what he did to Sheba."

"Honestly, Mrs Fitzherbert," Julie said, "I

really don't think Ben scared Sheba away."

For a moment Mrs Fitzherbert's eyes were icy cold. Then her face began to crumple. She pressed her lips together for a moment. Then she said, "No? Well, maybe you're right. Maybe Sheba has been stolen. In fact I'm sure of it. I'll probably get a ransom note quite soon now. I'll pay whatever they ask."

Neil watched as the old woman made her way wearily past them.

"She feels the same as me," he said. "She'd rather Sheba was stolen than lost."

"Poor Mrs Fitz," Julie said. "She really must love Sheba."

"I think she does," Emily said. "She was close to tears just then."

"I guess she's not so bad after all," Neil said. "Anybody who's as fond of a dog as that can't be all bad."

Ben was still pulling on his lead but Julie restrained him. "No, Ben," she said. "Mrs Fitz was looking down by the river. Sheba isn't there."

"We might as well go home," said Neil.

The others nodded and pulled their collars up against the icy wind. Neil looked up at the sky. It was heavy with snow. If Sheba was lying injured out in the open he was sure she wouldn't last the night.

Chapter Eight

It was nearly eight o'clock that evening when Julie rang again.

"Ben's missing," she said.

"*What?*" said Neil. "When? How?"

Julie was close to tears. "I don't know exactly," she said. "Mum and I were out. We left Ben at home. I think he must have got out through a downstairs window. Either that or somebody let him out."

"You mean Mrs Fitz?" Neil said.

"Who else?" said Julie.

"But why would she do that?" Neil asked.

Julie sighed. "Oh, I don't know. Maybe

I'm imagining things. I keep wondering if she drove him away somewhere in her car and dumped him. She hates him so much."

"Oh, Julie, no," Neil said. "You saw Mrs Fitz earlier on. You saw how upset she was about Sheba. Nobody that loves a dog so much could be cruel to another dog."

"You're probably right," Julie said. "But if you are, where is he?"

Neil was a long time on the phone. He called Emily to speak to Julie but neither of them could be of much help. It was dark already. There was no point in starting a search until morning.

"He'll turn up," Emily said to Julie. "Just wait and see. He'll arrive at the back door, covered in mud, and you'll give him a hug and everything will be all right."

Neil watched her put the phone down and turn to him. Her face didn't look nearly as confident as her voice had sounded.

Neil looked out of the window. The first flakes of snow were falling, drifting against the window pane. As he watched they got heavier – great fat flakes of snow, swirling in the light of the courtyard lamp.

Emily shivered. "I can't bear to think about it," she said. "Two dogs missing on a night like this."

"We'll start looking for Ben first thing in the morning," Neil said. "Before school."

"Right," said Emily. "Wake me as soon as it's light."

Neil made a dive for the phone when it rang early next morning. It had to be Julie, saying that Ben was safe at home.

"Hi," Hasheem said. "Great news. School's closed today because of the snow."

Neil's heart sank. "Is it that bad?" he said. He looked out of the window. The courtyard and garden were thickly covered with freshly fallen snow.

Hasheem laughed. "I wouldn't call it bad – not when it lets us off school for a day. Can you call Chris? And tell him to call Phil. We're doing a chain phone call so that everybody gets the message."

"Right," said Neil. "See you, Hasheem. Bye!"

Neil phoned Chris who said the road to Compton was under drifts of about a metre. "It's wild," he said. "They've got the snowploughs out. Do you fancy going sledging? Or skiing? A few of us are going to try to meet up."

"Not today, Chris," Neil said. "I've got things to do."

Like look for two dogs, Neil thought as he rang Julie's number.

Ben still hadn't appeared.

"We'll come right over and start searching," Neil said. "Dad will bring us. The

87

Range Rover won't have a problem with the roads."

"Are you warm enough?" Carole Parker said as they got ready to leave.

Neil and Emily looked at her. They were wearing bright ski jackets and chunky padded trousers.

"Of course we're warm enough," Neil said.

"Maybe we should take the skis," said Emily, pulling at her jacket. It was an old one of Steve's and a bit big for her.

Neil shook his head. "They wouldn't be any use," he said. "If we had cross-country skis it would be different."

"I'm going sledging," said Sarah.

"That's an idea," said Neil. "Let's take a sledge."

"What for?" said Emily.

Neil bit his lip. "Just in case," he said. He didn't want to say what was in his mind – *in case they found Ben unable to walk*. Neil had given up hope for Sheba. She would never have survived the night if she'd been out in the open. Even Ben with his thick coat would be in real trouble.

Bob Parker dropped them off at Julie's house. "I'd help you look," he said, "but there's such a lot to do at the kennels. For a start, I've got to clear the snow away from the runs and make sure the dogs are safely bedded down."

"That's OK, Dad," Neil said. "Thanks for bringing us."

"Ring if there's any news," Bob Parker said.

"We will," Emily said.

Neil looked across at Mrs Fitzherbert's house. The old lady was at the window, watching. Her face looked grey with tiredness and worry. Neil raised his hand and gave her a wave. Mrs Fitzherbert hesitated a moment, then she lifted her hand slightly before letting it drop back.

Julie came out of the house as Mr Parker drove off.

"Any news?" Emily asked.

Julie shook her head. "I've been out already across the playing fields," she said. "Nothing."

"There's no point in going by the road," Neil said. "Snowploughs have been out. If

he was anywhere along the road they'd
have found him and contacted you, Julie.
His collar's got his name and address on it,
hasn't it?"

Julie nodded. "That only leaves the wood
and the river again," she said.

"Let's go then," said Emily. "There's no
time to waste."

Neil, Emily and Julie trudged through
the deep snow past the school and down on
towards the river.

"Mrs Fitz looks terrible," Neil said.

Julie nodded. "She found a hole in the
hedge and a bit of Sheba's fur sticking to it.
Now she knows how Sheba got out."

"So she doesn't blame Ben any more?"
Emily said.

"No," said Julie. "But she's given up hope
for Sheba."

Neil didn't say anything. The sledge
skimmed the snow behind him. He couldn't
help thinking about what they might have
to bring back on it.

"We've been this way before," Emily
said as they came within sight of the
belt of trees down by the river. This is

where we met Mrs Fitz yesterday."

"Let's make for the bend in the river further down," Neil said. "Keep a lookout for tracks."

Emily shook her head. "The snow is too fresh," she said. "And anyway, it's started snowing again. Any tracks will be covered up in no time."

They trudged on, knee-deep in snow in some places, shouting, whistling, calling Ben until they were hoarse.

"What was that?" said Julie.

"What?" said Neil.

"I heard something," Julie said.

"I didn't hear anything," said Emily.

"Shush," said Julie. "Listen!"

Far away, to their left and behind them, came a deep booming sound.

"It's Ben," said Julie, her face lighting up. "It's Ben! I'd know his bark anywhere."

Chapter Nine

Neil turned and looked round the snow-covered fields. "Where did the barking come from?" he said. "Try shouting again, Julie. Call his name."

They made their way back the way they had come, calling Ben and stopping every so often to get their bearings.

"That way," said Julie, pointing towards the belt of trees.

"That's where Mrs Fitzherbert was looking yesterday," said Emily.

Julie nodded. "And it's where Ben got really excited, remember? Come on!"

Stumbling in the deep, soft snow, they

plodded towards the trees. The snow had started to fall again in great fat flakes, stinging their eyes, coating their eyelashes so that they could hardly see. All the time the resonant booming of Ben's bark got louder and louder as they got nearer the woods.

Tripping through the trees on snow-laden roots and losing their footing in sudden hollows, they were now almost at the river's edge. A fallen tree loomed up before them, hanging out over the river, its roots torn from the earth.

The snow was falling so thickly that it took Neil a moment to make out the shape huddled under the gaping tree roots. The dead tree was a metre or so above the river and the upended tree root formed a wind-break. Snow lay piled up against it but there was a more protected hollow in the lee of the tree roots. There, lying in the hollow, was Ben.

His white head and chest merged with the snow so that, for a moment, only the blue-grey of his coat showed, encrusted with snow.

"There he is," Julie yelled. "There's Ben!"

She climbed over the snow-covered tree roots and dropped into the hollow.

Neil was next to arrive, panting from the effort of running in deep snow. He wiped his hand across his eyes as he looked at Ben. He could just see a patch of darker grey on Ben's white chest. He looked again, unable to believe his eyes.

Ben lay under the shelter of the tree roots, his huge front paws crossed in front of him and his body curved protectively round his forelegs. As Neil and Emily reached him, Ben raised his head, whimpering, and looked at them as if to say, "What took you so long?" Then he bent his head down again and licked the small bundle he held between his forelegs.

"It's Sheba," Julie said softly.

"Is she alive?" Neil asked.

Julie took off her mittens and laid a hand on the small body. She nodded. "Her body's warm and I can feel her heart beating. But there's something wrong with her. She's lying awkwardly." She felt further down. "Her leg is caught under a tree root,"

94

she said. "We'll have to be careful about moving her."

"That must be why Ben had to stay with her," Emily said. "He couldn't leave her and she couldn't move. He's been keeping her warm."

Neil laid a hand on Ben's coat. It was thick with snow and the ends were stiff with ice. He dug deeper, down into the undercoat. There was warmth there still but Ben was losing heat fast.

"We have to get them back as quickly as possible," he said, unwinding his scarf. He started to rub Ben's coat, loosening the frost on it, rubbing warmth back into the dog's body, trying to stimulate his circulation.

"I'll help," said Julie, taking off her own scarf.

"Emily, you take Sheba," Neil said, thinking fast. "Put her inside your ski jacket – it's big enough. But be careful how you lift her – mind her leg."

For a moment Emily studied the tree root that held Sheba's leg. "I need something to lever that tree root up," she said.

Julie picked up a fallen branch, shaking the snow off it. "How about this?" she asked.

"That looks just the thing," Emily said. "If you could keep Sheba still, I'll give it a try."

Julie put her hands round Sheba's small body, soothing her. The little dog looked up at her and tried to bark but she could only manage a squeak.

Emily wedged the branch under the tree root. Then, very gently, she levered it to one side while Julie lifted the little dog into her arms.

"Oh," said Emily, examining Sheba's leg. "She's hurt, she's injured."

"Badly?" asked Neil, still rubbing Ben's coat.

Emily shook her head. "I can't tell," she said. "But we'd better get her home fast."

"What about Ben?" Julie said, coming to help Neil. "He can't walk all that way." Then her face cleared. "Of course, the sledge. We can take him on the sledge! That was good thinking, Neil."

Neil beamed. He thought so too – now that they would be taking home two live dogs.

It wasn't easy to load Ben onto the sledge. He was very cold indeed and weakened after a night in the open. Even after a good rub-down, he was still so stiff he could hardly stand, much less walk.

"Come on, Ben. Come on, boy," Julie said softly, putting her arms around him. "Not far to go. Just onto the sledge. You can do it, boy. Come on."

Neil held his breath. Ben had to do it. There was no way they could lift his weight onto the sledge. They would be able to pull

97

the sledge easily enough once they got it moving, but Ben had to do this part himself.

"Now, Ben, please try!" Julie said, her face tight with unshed tears.

Slowly Ben lumbered to his feet, moving so stiffly it must have been painful for him. Neil brought the sledge as close as he could. Julie put her arms round Ben's neck.

"Come on, Ben," she said. "You have to get onto the sledge."

Ben raised his big shaggy head and looked at her. Julie tugged on his collar.

"Come on, Ben – please," she said, tears sliding down her face.

Ben looked at the sledge and slowly put out a paw.

"That's it! Good boy, Ben," Julie encouraged him.

Ben made a huge effort and climbed heavily onto the sledge with Julie guiding him.

"Sit now, Ben," she said. "Lie down."

The big bobtail sank down onto the sledge, exhausted.

Julie took off her anorak and spread it over him, tucking it round him. Ben lifted his head slightly and licked her hand.

"You'll get soaked," Neil said. "You'll freeze!"

But Julie's face was shining. "I won't even feel the cold," she said. "I'm so happy I could *fly* home. I feel amazing!"

And she *was* amazing. It was as if she had twice her normal strength. Emily gave the sledge a push to start it off and Julie and Neil dragged it across the snow, setting up a pace that made it easier to pull.

Emily had little Sheba tucked inside her jacket. The tiny dog was too weak to protest and lay there, snugly, happy to be out of the cold.

Mrs Baker and Mrs Fitzherbert heard them coming even before they got to the garden gate. They both came running to their back doors.

"We've found them. Mrs Fitzherbert, we've got Sheba. She's alive. Ben saved her!"

Mrs Fitzherbert ran out into the snow

and stood there, just looking, not able to believe her eyes, as Emily opened her ski jacket. Sheba's little face peered out.

"Sheba," Mrs Fitzherbert whispered. She swayed and Julie's mum ran to her.

"What are you doing out in the snow in your slippers?" she said, ignoring her own slippers. "Come into the house."

In moments they were gathered round the fire, the two dogs huddled together once more in front of the heat.

"You get towels, I'll get some food," Emily said to Julie and Neil.

Julie fetched two enormous thick bath towels for Ben and a smaller, softer towel for Sheba, and she and Neil gave the dogs a good rub-down. Ben was already beginning to look more like himself as the heat from the fire warmed him, and Julie's rubbing brought back the circulation.

Neil finished rubbing Sheba down and laid her carefully in Mrs Fitzherbert's lap. The old lady's eyes overflowed with tears.

"Now, Mrs Fitzherbert," Neil teased, "don't you go getting her wet when I've just dried her."

Mrs Fitzherbert laughed and brushed away the tears. "Tell me all about it," she said. "Tell me about finding her – oh, I can't tell you how grateful I am."

They explained how they had searched for Ben.

"The dogs were right down by the river – where you were yesterday," Emily said.

"I didn't get as far as the river," Mrs Fitzherbert said. "I heard you coming and turned back."

"So Ben really did get excited because he

scented Sheba," Julie said. "We thought he started barking because he saw you."

"And that brave dog went back for my Sheba," Mrs Fitzherbert said.

"Just as soon as he could," Neil said.

"I can't believe it," said Mrs Fitzherbert.

"He's a sheepdog," Julie said. "It's in his blood. He'd curled himself around Sheba just the way he would have done with a puppy or a newborn lamb."

Neil smiled. "I suppose Sheba must *seem* like a newborn lamb to Ben – she's just about the right size."

"Ben may not be a showdog," said Emily. "He might not ever win any prizes. But he's a really great sheepdog."

Mrs Fitzherbert looked at Ben. "You don't have to be a pedigree to be a truly great dog," she said. "And that's what Ben is – he's the best!"

"How is Sheba?" Neil asked. "Emily said she was hurt."

Mrs Fitzherbert examined Sheba. "Her leg seems to be painful," she said. "It's grazed and sore but I don't think it's broken. I'll ask the vet to check her anyway."

"Her leg was caught under a tree root," Neil said. "She couldn't get free. That's why Ben had to stay with her and keep her warm."

Mrs Fitzherbert looked around at all of them. "I've been so nasty to you," she said. "I'm so ashamed of myself."

Mrs Baker came into the room carrying a tray laden with tea and freshly baked scones. Neil suddenly realized how hungry he was.

"Now, none of that," Julie's mum said to Mrs Fitzherbert. "That's all water under the bridge. We got off to a bad start but I can tell we're going to be good neighbours after all." She hesitated, then said, "I promise to get that fence fixed just as soon as possible."

Mrs Fitzherbert looked at Sheba and Ben. "Oh, there's no hurry," she said. "Ben is welcome in my garden any time." Then she turned to Neil, Julie and Emily. "And you can call me 'Mrs Fitz'," she said. "That's what my friends call me."

Neil, Julie and Emily looked at one another and tried not to giggle.

"Oh, we call you that already," said Julie.

Mrs Fitzherbert looked surprised. Then she smiled. "That means we're already friends," she said.

Chapter Ten

Mrs Fitzherbert started bringing Sheba over to King Street for obedience classes. The little dog was nervous at first but, as long as Ben was around, she behaved well and very soon Neil began to see a difference in her.

"Look at Sheba," Kate McGuire, the kennel maid, said to Neil on the Saturday before the show.

Sheba and Ben were playing together in the courtyard at King Street while Mrs Fitzherbert was in the office having a word with Mrs Parker.

Neil grinned. "You'd never think she was the same dog, would you?" he said. "She's had a real personality change – thanks to Ben."

Julie laughed. "Not entirely," she said. "She can still put Ben in his place if he gets too rough."

"Sheba could put a tiger in its place," Emily said. "It's funny. Ben is a real softie and Sheba would stand up to anything."

"But she doesn't mind other dogs now," said Kate. "And that *is* thanks to Ben. I love seeing those two together."

"They're inseparable," said Julie. "Mrs Fitz says she doesn't want the fence mended. That way they can run back and forth between the gardens."

Kate pushed her long blonde hair back from her face. "I just wish we'd had as much luck with Finn," she said.

Neil frowned. "Isn't he going to be able to compete at the show?"

Kate shook her head. "I don't think so," she said. "I haven't had much success with him. He's trying to boss the other dogs around. You can't have that sort of behaviour at a show where there are lots of dogs."

Finn had come to King Street for a few days as Mr Parker had suggested. But if Kate couldn't work the magic on him, nobody could. Kate was a natural with dogs.

"Dr Harvey is coming to pick him up," Kate said, looking at her watch. "He should be here any minute. I'll go and fetch Finn."

"Poor Dr Harvey," Emily said. "He'll be so disappointed."

"Poor Finn," Neil replied. "If he doesn't get out of this habit of defending his territory soon, he might never get over it."

"Guess what?" shouted a voice from the house and Sarah came running across the courtyard with Sam at her heels. Mrs Fitzherbert was behind her with Mrs Parker.

Neil bent to give Sam a rub. At least *he* was ready for the Manchester show. He was performing really well on the Agility course.

"What?" said Emily to Sarah.

"Mrs Fitzherbert wants Ben to come to

the show with Sheba," Sarah said. "So we'll all be going. Sam and Ben and Sheba – and us, of course."

Julie gasped. "*Ben!*" she said. "Can you imagine Ben at a dog show?"

Ben looked up at the sound of his name. Sam barked and made off across the courtyard with Ben at his heels. Just at that moment Dr Harvey drove into the driveway and Kate came out of kennel block two with Finn.

Finn strained at his lead and Kate unclipped it so that the Kerry blue could run and meet his owner.

Sam stopped short and whirled round as Finn raced across the courtyard. At once the collie backed away. Sam had learned to back off when Finn was around – just like Sandy. But Ben didn't care. Big, friendly Ben lolloped over to Finn and stopped right in front of him – between the Kerry blue and Dr Harvey.

Finn stopped, hackles rising and forelegs stiffening. He gave a long, low growl and Ben shook his head and butted him playfully on the nose. Finn snarled.

"Finn!" said Dr Harvey sharply.

But before Dr Harvey could reach him, a small grey bundle of energy threw itself between the two dogs.

"Sheba!" Mrs Fitzherbert called. "Oh, no! Come back, Sheba."

Mrs Parker laid a hand on her arm. "Wait," she said. "Look!"

They all watched the dogs. Sam was standing to one side, looking interested. Ben looked a bit puzzled as he began to back away. But Sheba stood her ground as Finn growled at her. She gave a short, sharp bark and Finn stopped growling.

Step by step Sheba advanced on the Kerry blue, forcing him back, away from Ben.

"She's protecting Ben," Neil said.

"She's doing more than that," said Mrs Parker. "She's making Finn give way."

They watched as the Kerry blue moved steadily back, his eyes locked on Sheba's. Then, all of a sudden, Finn dropped his hindquarters and lay down in front of the little poodle. Sheba stepped towards him daintily and laid a tiny paw on his flank.

"Good gracious," Mrs Parker said. "You know what that means in doggy language, don't you?"

Neil laughed. "It means 'I'm the boss'," he said.

Dr Harvey walked across to them. "You were right, Neil," he said. "Sheba *is* a match for Finn."

Mrs Parker looked thoughtful. "If you aren't in a hurry," she said to Dr Harvey, "I think this might be the time to start working on Finn."

"Strike while the iron is hot?" said Dr Harvey, grinning.

"Exactly," said Mrs Parker. "It's too good an opportunity to miss."

Mrs Parker turned to Mrs Fitzherbert. "Can we borrow Sheba for half an hour?" she said. "Just in case Finn gets out of line again."

Mrs Fitzherbert flushed with pleasure. "Of course you can," she said. "Anything to help."

Neil, Julie and Emily looked at one another. Ben had solved Sheba's problem. Now it looked as if Sheba was going to solve Finn's.

Kate grinned. "Keep your fingers crossed," she said. "We might see Finn at the show after all."

"Wow!" said Neil, looking round the show ring. "Look at all these dogs, Sam."

The collie wagged his tail. He seemed to be enjoying himself amongst all the people and other dogs.

"Where's Mrs Fitz?" Julie asked, holding tightly to Ben's lead. Ben wanted to make friends with every dog he saw – and there were a lot of dogs!

"There she is," Sarah said. "She's just getting ready to show Sheba."

Neil, Julie, Emily and Sarah made their way over to the ringside of another arena nearby where Mrs Fitzherbert was giving Sheba a last brush.

"You know, Sheba has never actually won a prize before," Mrs Fitzherbert said. "She's always been a little nervous of the other dogs."

Neil gave Sheba a pat. The little dog stood perfectly still, eyes alert.

"She isn't nervous today," he said.

Mrs Fitzherbert smiled. "Thanks to King Street Kennels and Ben," she said. "And, do you know, I don't mind at all about her winning a prize today. It's so lovely to see her happy and confident amongst all these other dogs."

"There's the announcement, Mrs Fitz," Emily said as the loudspeaker crackled into life. "You're on!"

"I can't bear to watch," Julie said. "I never thought a show would be this nerve-racking."

Neil looked at his watch. He had fifteen

minutes before the Agility trials started. He felt more nervous than he ever had before. This was Sam's first appearance at a big dog show and Neil desperately wanted to do well.

"Here comes Dr Harvey," Emily said. Her face broke into a wide grin. "His competition must be over."

They all turned to watch Dr Harvey lead Finn over to them. Sandy trotted near him on his other side.

"I couldn't believe how well behaved he was," he said proudly, looking down at his Kerry blue.

"Oh, Finn, well done," Neil said, bending down to give the dog a hug. He looked up at Dr Harvey. "No problems?"

"He was as good as gold," Dr Harvey said.

"And how is Sandy?" Emily said, bending down to give Sandy a cuddle.

"He's fine," said Dr Harvey. "In fact, he and Finn are getting on like a house on fire. I must tell your parents. Where are they?"

Julie pointed to the other side of the

ring. "They're over there with my mum," she said.

"Thanks. I'm off then. Hope Sam does well." He walked away into the crowd.

The people round the ring suddenly burst into loud applause.

"What's happening?" said Emily.

"Look, it's Sheba. She's doing really well," Neil said, his eyes on the little dog. "Look at her standing perfectly still. No nerves."

"Do we know who's won yet?" asked Julie.

Neil craned his neck to see which dog was getting the rosette for first place. The loudspeaker announced the name of an unfamiliar dog, and then two other names they didn't know for second and third.

"I hope she won't be too disappoint—" said Emily.

"Hang on, there's another prize," interrupted Neil.

"And Sheba of Sharendon," the loudspeaker said, "is awarded a special mention for appearance and manner."

"I don't believe it," Emily said.

"Mrs Fitz will be over the moon," said Neil.

The loudspeaker crackled into life again.

"That's the call for the Agility event," Emily said.

Neil clutched Sam's lead tightly. "I'd better go," he said. We can meet Mum and Dad there."

They made their way back through the crowds to where the Agility course was set up. Neil swallowed hard as he looked at it again. It looked even more alarming than when he had walked round it earlier.

The competitors were lining up. As Neil joined them he saw his parents and Mrs Baker arrive. He waved and they gave him a thumbs-up for luck.

Sam was fifth to go. Neil's mouth was dry as he watched the other dogs. The first, a German shepherd, looked as if he was going to get a clear round but he missed one of the tyres. Then came a young Labrador who was fast but didn't manage to touch all the contact points on the course.

Neil was a bit worried about the contact points. Sam liked the Agility course so much he was reluctant to stop long enough to make contact with the yellow squares on various obstacles. Neil watched as a spaniel and a Skye terrier ran the course. They both dropped ten penalty points. Then it was Sam's turn.

As Neil led him to the starting point, he saw Mrs Fitzherbert arrive with Dr Harvey.

"Come on, Sam," he whispered. "Everybody's rooting for you."

Then Sam was off, racing for the tube, wriggling through it, across the dog walk, through the first hanging tyre, over the bridge which crossed a trough of plants and flowers, down the tunnel to the first contact point.

"Stay, Sam," Neil whispered under his breath.

Sam touched the contact point – and stayed.

Then he was off again. Through the fixed tyre, over the see-saw, balancing well, and another contact point touched. Then the barrel and, looming ahead, the steps. Sam slowed, hesitated. Neil's heart sank. Was he going to refuse?

Then Sam gathered his haunches and leapt for the first step. Up he went, down the other side. Only the final race to the finish line now.

But Sam turned and looked at Neil as if to say, "I did it." Neil bit his lip. Sam wagged his tail then turned and ran for the finish. But he had lost precious moments and he would be penalized for stopping.

Suddenly, as Sam crossed the line, it didn't matter. Sam had done brilliantly. He had touched the contact points, taken every obstacle – and he had thoroughly enjoyed it. Neil threw his arms round Sam's neck.

"Well done, boy," he said. "Well done!"

Sarah was first to arrive, hugging Neil and Sam. Neil looked up as the others came rushing up, full of congratulations.

"I told you he wouldn't disgrace you," Dr Harvey said.

Neil grinned.

Julie and Ben raced up, the big Old English sheepdog obviously very excited and itching to join in the fun. As Julie reached down to congratulate Sam, Ben tugged his lead free and tore off through the crowds, heading straight for a large Labrador in one of the show tents nearby.

"No, Ben, no!" Julie yelled.

Neil watched in horror as Ben raced straight through the open entrance and made to leap over a display inside. Unfortunately, he didn't manage to clear it and landed amongst the plants and flowers. Every dog in the area started barking.

Mrs Baker and Julie ran across the course to collect Ben while Mr Parker tried to calm the officials down. By the time the

Bakers got back with Ben, Bob had sorted things out.

"I reckon they think we're all mad," Bob Parker said.

"Trust Ben to get all excited and cause trouble!" said Julie.

The loudspeaker burst into life.

"It's the Agility course results," Emily said, grabbing Neil's arm.

Neil listened, hardly breathing. The German shepherd was first. Another Border collie second. "Third – Neilsboy Puppy Patrol Sam!"

"He got a prize," yelled Neil. "He came third. That's brilliant. He'll get a rosette."

Mr Parker smiled. "You don't need a rosette to prove that you're a great dog, Sam," he said as everyone crowded round, congratulating Neil.

"You certainly don't," said Mrs Fitzherbert. "But there's one dog here that really does deserve a rosette."

She bent down and unpinned Sheba's rosette. Then she pinned it on Ben's collar.

Neil looked at the huge Old English sheepdog, bits of flowers and plants sticking

119

out of his shaggy coat. He had to be the scruffiest dog in history to get a rosette at a dog show.

"It's the prize for the best dressed dog," he joked.

"Not at all," said Mrs Fitzherbert. "Ben's prize is just for being Ben."

"Oh, he's good at that," said Julie, giving Ben a cuddle. "He's *very* good at being Ben."

Look out for the third brilliant Puppy Patrol title

Abandoned!
Jenny Dale

"**W**ell, I think we can safely say that Mr Harding's not going to come for Jessie tonight," Bob Parker announced late that evening. "I've just tried that telephone number he gave us. I got the 'number unobtainable' sound, so I checked with the operator. It's out of order, according to her."

Neil bit his lip. Should he tell his dad what he and Kate had found out about Harding's address?

For the moment he decided to keep quiet. He wanted to work it out himself, and with everything else that had happened, the matter of 149 Dale End Road had slipped his mind. Anyway, they had all felt so positive that Harding *would* be back to pick up Jessie.

"What do we do now, then?" Neil enquired.

"Wait to see if he turns up tomorrow. He's probably had some unavoidable delay."

Neil hoped his father was right – that it wasn't anything more serious than that . . .

PUPPY PATROL titles available from Macmillan Children's Books

The prices shown below are correct at the time of going to press. However, Macmillan Publishers reserve the right to show new retail prices on covers which may differ from those previously advertised.

JENNY DALE

1. Teacher's Pet	0 330 34905 8	£2.99
2. Big Ben	0 330 34906 6	£2.99
3. Abandoned!	0 330 34907 4	£2.99
4. Double Trouble	0 330 34908 2	£2.99
5. Star Paws	0 330 34909 0	£2.99
6. Tug of Love	0 330 34910 4	£2.99
7. Saving Skye	0 330 35492 2	£2.99
8. Tuff's Luck	0 330 35493 0	£2.99

All Macmillan titles can be ordered at your local bookshop or are available by post from:

**Book Service by Post
PO Box 29, Douglas, Isle of Man IM99 1BQ**

Credit cards accepted. For details:
Telephone: 01624 675137
Fax: 01624 670923
E-mail: bookshop@enterprise.net

Free postage and packing in the UK.
Overseas customers: add £1 per book (paperback)
and £3 per book (hardback).